MIKE THALER PRESENTS ...

ACTION HEROES OF THE BIBLE

THE SERMONATORS

5

FUN BIBLE STORIES

BY MIKE THALER
ILLUSTRATIONS BY DENNIS ADLER

Faith KiD

Equipping Kids fo
Faithkids.com

D1440803

Faith Building Guide

Youth/ Children

Obedience

A Faith Building Guide can be found on page 32.

Dedicated to Jan Dennis
whose laughter punctuates these stories.
Mike

Faith Kids® is an imprint of
Cook Communications, Colorado Springs, Colorado 80918
Cook Communications, Paris, Ontario
Kingsway Communications, Eastbourne, England

ACTION HEROES OF THE BIBLE
© 2002 by Mike Thaler for text and Dennis Adler for illustrations

Published in association with the literary agency of Alive Communications, Inc.,
7680 Goddard St., Suite 200, Colorado Springs CO 80920.

Edited by Heather Gemmen
Designed by Clyde Van Cleve

First printing, 2002
Printed in Singapore
06 05 04 03 02   5 4 3 2 1

Library of Congress Cataloging-in-Publication

Thaler, Mike, 1936-
   Action heroes of the Bible : the sermonators / by Mike Thaler ; illustrated by Dennis Adler.
      p. cm. --
   Summary: Five comical retelling of Bible stories demonstrate God's willingness to
   forgive over and over again.
   ISBN 0-7814-3649-4
   1. Bible stories, English--O.T. 2. Bible. O.T.--Juvenile humor. [1. Bible stories--O.T.]
I. Adler, Dennis (Dennis H.), 1942-ill. II Title.

BS551.3 .T45 2002
221.9'505--dc21

                                        2001055676

Mike Thaler Presents . . .

- Action Heroes of the Bible: The Sermonators
- Prophets of the Bible: God's Anchormen
- Heroines of the Bible: God's Fair Ladies

Books in the Heaven and Mirth® Series:

- Adam and the Apple Turnover
- Moses: Take Two Tablets and Call Me in the Morning
- The Prodigal Son: Oh Brother
- Daniel: Nice Kitty!
- David & Bubblebath Sheba
- David: God's Rock Star
- Elijah: Prophet Sharing
- John the Baptist, Wet & Wild
- Paul: God's Message Sent Apostle Post

4

Othniel
We Deliver

THE ISRAELITES
needed glasses.
They lost sight of what God
wanted them to do,
and did what was right
in their own eyes.
However, all of them
were *myopic*.
They made spectacles
of themselves.
They started serving other gods.
They put up idols:
gold lions with chicken feet,
hippos with the heads of ducks,
and CPAs with the heads of hamsters.
It was a real mess.

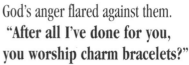

God's anger flared against them. **"After all I've done for you, you worship charm bracelets?"**

So he delivered them
into the hateful hands
of their enemy: C.R. *
king of Aram.
For eight years
they suffered
under his cruel rule.
Finally they cried out
to the Almighty One and Only.
"Lord, deliver us
from this malace in the palace."
And God heard their plea
and sent Othniel to set them free.

Othniel, whose nickname was "Oatmeal,"
was a stick-to-the-ribs guy.
His uncle Caleb was courageous
and had always remained
faithful to the Lord.
Othniel grew up hearing
the great battle stories of Israel.
So the Spirit of the Lord
came upon Othniel
and he became Israel's general judge.

* Cruel Ruler

He defeated King C.R. of Aram,
  really did scare'em,
  didn't spare'em,
  and killed him in his harem.
So the Israelites
  were free again,
  and there was peace
  for forty years.
With much fanfare,
  Othniel was inducted into
  the Deliverers' Hall of Fame
  along with Moses
and Joshua
and his uncle Caleb.

THE END

Nuggets from Goldie, the miner prophet:
*"God will always give you a second chance
to make a first impression."*

For the real story, read Judges 3:7–11.

Ehud
The Quickest Sword in the Negev

ONCE AGAIN
the Israelites became smog
in the eyes of God.
This time he FedEx'd® them
into the hands of their enemies–
the Moabites.
They were ruled
by King Eglon the Fat
for eighteen years.
Now Eglon was a real wide load.
His robes were made
by Omar the tentmaker.

He didn't know when to stop eating.
He always took just one *Moabite*.
The Israelites finally got tired
of feeding him
so they cried out to the Lord.
"Lord, save us from this lard!"
And God heard them—
and gave them Ehud.
Now Ehud was left-handed
and had a trick sword.
It was sharpened on both sides
and he wore it in a quick draw
holster hidden under his tunic.

"Can you save us?"
cried the Israelites.

"I'll take a stab at it,"
smiled Ehud.

Now Ehud had a plan.
He got a job at Pizza Hut®
and when King Eglon
ordered thirty thick-crust pizzas
with everything—for a snack—
Ehud delivered them.
Palace security was not so tight
in those days

10

and he easily got by the metal detector.
Eglon was tucking a napkin under his chin
going "yum, yum, yum."
After Ehud delivered the pizzas—still hot—
he whispered in Eglon's ear,
"I have a secret message for you."

"I just love secret messages,"
gurgled Eglon,
devouring the first pizza,
box and all.
He sent away
all his attendants
and leaned forward.

"Let's have it," he whispered.

"It's a message from God,"
Ehud started.

"Give it to me straight," said Eglon.

So Ehud took out his sword
and gave it to him straight.
It went so far into Eglon
that it disappeared, handle and all.
"Get the point?" chuckled Ehud,
and he locked all the doors
and jumped out the window.

11

An hour later the servants came
and found the doors locked.

"He's just digesting," they laughed,
for they called him the *court digester*.

"Or he's on the throne," they giggled.

But after ten hours
they began to worry.
They got the pass key
and opened the door.
There they found
their king dead,
with a very surprised look
on his face.
They couldn't find the sword
so they just figured
he choked on a pizza box.
Even the coroner
missed the sword
and attributed his death
to natural causes.

In the meantime,
Ehud rallied the Israelites
and they captured the bridge
to Moab during rush hour

and struck down
ten thousand
Moabite commuters,
taking a heavy toll.
That day Israel triumphed
over Moab,
and there was peace
for eighty years.
A grateful people
gave Ehud a new sword
and inducted him
into the Deliverers' Hall of Fame.

THE END

Nuggets from Goldie, the miner prophet:
*"Sometimes when you give God orders,
you get stuck with the bill,"*

For the real story, read Judges 3:12–30.

13

Shamgar
A Hands-on Deliverer

GOD HAD COMMANDED
the Israelites to extinguish
all the other *lites,*
ites, and *ines.*
But they did not obey Him,
and the Canaanites
and the Philistines
took over the land.
The Israelites just
snuck around in alleys

or stayed tense
in their tents.
God wanted them
to get out more,
so he sent Shamgar
the Invincible.
Although he had a good name,
he didn't have a good press agent,
so there isn't much
written about him.

Also, he didn't have
a trick weapon
or even a trick.
But when the Lord
is with you,
you don't need one.
Shamgar was from the school
of hard knocks.
He swung into action
and racked up six hundred
Philistines with a pool cue.*
He cleared the table
and saved Israel from being stuck
behind the eight ball.
After his death, he too was inducted
into the Deliverers' Hall of Fame,
and mentioned briefly
in a Bible camp song.

THE END

Nuggets from Goldie, the miner prophet:
*"When you're armed with the Spirit of God,
you don't need much else."*

For the real story, read Judges 3:31.

*really an ox goad

Gideon

Here Comes the Judge

ALTHOUGH GOD GAVE THE ISRAELITES
many signs, they still kept straying off the path
of righteousness. They started worshipping
lawn trolls and pink flamingos.
They were carrying rabbits' feet
and putting horseshoes on their doors.
This made God very unhappy.
So He set the Midianites upon them.
Now the Midianites were worse
than termites; they ate the Jews
out of house and home.
The poor Israelites
had to go live in caves.
Things got so bad
they finally cried out
to the Lord:

"Knock knock."

"Who's there?"

"Midianite."

"Midianite who?"

"We've spent *Midianite* oppressed by them!"

God sent them a telegram:

I TOOK YOU OUT OF SLAVERY IN EGYPT STOP
I DEFEATED ALL YOUR ENEMIES
AND GAVE YOU THEIR LANDS STOP
AND THIS IS THE THANKS I GET STOP
YOU BOW DOWN BEFORE HORSESHOES STOP
Signed: **The Lord Your God.**

But the Lord's heart softened.
He sent an angel to talk to Gideon.
"Yo, Gideon. You're the man—the Lord is with you."

"Hey, if the Lord is with me, why are things so bad?"

"Listen up," said the angel.
"You have been chosen to drive out the Midianites."

"Why me?" sighed Gideon.
"I'm known as Gideon the Puny."

"Puny or not," exclaimed the angel,

"your name rhymes with Midian, so you're the guy!"

"Look," said Gideon. "If you really mean me,
give me a sign. Wait here, I'll be right back."

"Okay," said the Lord, **"but hurry up,
I've got a universe to run."**

So Gideon ran and killed a goat
and made some bread and soup for lunch.
He brought it out to the angel.

"I've got a 2:30 appointment,"
the angel said, looking at his watch.
"Put the soup and the bread on this rock."
Gideon did and the angel touched it with his wing tip—
and it disappeared in flames.
Then the angel disappeared too.

"Hey," said Gideon. "That really *was* God."

"Cool it, man," said a voice from heaven.

That night God spoke to Gideon again.
**"Gideon, go to the front lawn
of your father's house and tip over
all the trolls and flamingos."**

"What about the polka dot
mushrooms and the teddy bears?"

"Them too. *Gideon* your way."

So Gideon got up at midnight
    (not to be confused with Midianite)
        and tipped over all his dad's lawn stuff.

In the morning
    when the neighbors
        saw what he had done
            they wanted to kill him.
                But his dad said,
                    "Look, let the gods of the
                    polka dot mushrooms
                    punish him."

"Cool," said the neighbors
and they went home.
But soon all the Midianites,
and all the other *ites* and *mites*,
gathered together
in one great army.

The Spirit of the Lord
came upon Gideon.
"This is it, boy. Go get'em!"

"There's a lot of them, Lord.
Look, I'll put down this sheepskin.
If You can make it wet
and keep the ground dry,
I'll know You mean business."

NEW SALEM MISSIONARY BAPTIST CHURCH
YOUTH & YOUNG ADULT REVIVAL

We Want GOD!

Featuring:

National Recording Artist
Leon Timbo

National Recording Artist
Nia Allen

Amazing Worship Experiences

The Bravest Young Voices in Columbus, OH

As a deer longs for flowing streams, so my soul longs for you, O God. My soul thirsts for God, for the living God. When shall I come and behold the face of God?" - Psalm 42:1-2

July 17-20, 2011
Sunday Services at 7:30 am & 10:45 am
Weeknights beginning at 6:30 pm

For more information or to participate contact 614-930-2242 or tsheppard@newsalemcares.com.
New Salem Missionary Baptist Church, Dr. Keith A. Troy, Pastor, 2956 Cleveland Ave. Columbus, OH 43224 www.newsalemcares.org

So the Lord did.

"There's really a lot of them, Lord.
Let's try two out of three.
I'll put the sheepskin down again.
If You can keep it dry
and make the ground wet,
I'll *really* know You mean business."

So the Lord did.

"Okay," said Gideon. "We'll go fight 'em."

"Wait," said the Lord.
"You have too many soldiers."

"Lord, you can never have too many soldiers."

"Send half of them home."

"Gee, Lord. Okay." So Gideon sent half of them home.
"Okay, Lord. Now we'll go fight 'em."

"Wait," said the Lord.
"You still have too many soldiers."

"But, Lord," gulped Gideon.
"There's an awful lot of Midianites."

"Send half of them home."

"Gee, Lord. Oh, okay."
So Gideon sent half of the remaining soldiers home.

"Can we go now, Lord?"

"You still have too many soldiers."

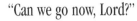

"Oh, come on, Lord.
There is just me and a few other guys!"

**"Take them down to the pool
to drink. Those that drink
with their noses shall go home.
Those that drink with their mouths
shall fight."**

So Gideon did what the Lord said.
Then he took his little band
and marched to the Midianite camp.

Instead of swords, the Lord gave Gideon
and his buddies trumpets.
Instead of spears, he gave them torches with pots on top.

"Can't we have arrows or something sharp?" asked Gideon.

"No," said the Lord. **"Blow your trumpets,
then uncover your torches."**

"Okay, Lord. I guess You know what You're doin'."
So they blew their trumpets and uncovered their torches—
and the Midianites were so confused
they ran around killing each other.

"See," said God.

"I knew it all the time," said Gideon,
who was getting more confident by the minute.

And so the Midianites were defeated
and the Israelites wanted to make Gideon
emperor, or king, or den father,
or *something*.

"Rule over us," they all cried.

"Not me," said Gideon.
"Only the Lord your God
can rule over you.
But there is one thing you can do for me.
You could each give me a gold earring."

So Gideon collected many gold earrings
which he later sold to print Bibles
that he placed by beds in motel rooms.

Amen!

THE END

Nuggets from Goldie, the miner prophet:
"When God intervenes on your account, you can bank on Him."

For the real story, read Judges 6–7.

SHELLY
SELLS
SEA
SHELLS

Jephthah
Man's Best Friend

WHEN LEFT TO THEIR OWN DEVICES,
the Israelites messed up again.
They started worshipping every other god
they could find. They even ordered
from god catalogs.
They had every idol, statue,
key chain, and bumper sticker
you could get.

This made the Lord's heart sad.
His wrath came down upon them
so all their enemies triumphed.

And, of course, they cried out
once again to the Lord—
who by this time had really had it.

"I've always saved you in the past,
but you guys never learn.
This time you're on your own.
Go ask one of your
coffee mugs for help."

"Please help us just
one more time.
We'll be good, God. Honest!"
cried the Israelites.

So God's heart softened
and He raised up another mighty warrior
His name was Jephthah.
His father was Gilead and his mother was Dubious,
so his family had driven him away.
Now in times of trouble they came to him and begged,
"Save us and we'll make you our leader."

"Really?" said Jephthah.

"Honest," they promised.
"Cross our hearts and hope to die."

So Jephthah returned with them and took command.

The king of the Ammonites sent him a message:
"Give us back our land."

"Hey," replied Jephthah,
"it's not *your* land anymore.

Our God gave it to *us*.
  And what God has put together
    let no man take away."
      And then the Lord moved Jephthah
      against the Ammonites.
      Before going into battle
      Jephthah made a vow:
      "Lord, if we win today,
      I will sacrifice to you
      whoever comes out of my house
    first to greet me."
  He was thinking his dog Spot
  would run out and jump upon him.
  But, instead, when he returned in triumph,
  his daughter ran out before the dog.

"Welcome home, Dad," she sang
  as she danced around him.

Jephthah fell on the ground
and tore his clothes.

  "Aren't you glad to see me, Dad?" she asked.

  "Oh, my daughter!
  You have broken my heart,
  for I have made a vow to God
    to sacrifice whoever greets me first."

  "Well, Dad, you have to keep your word.

29

A promise is a promise.
Just give me two months
to go cry with my girlfriends
because I will never date, get married,
and give you grand kids."

Jephthah, who felt rotten,
gave her three months
of pajama parties.
When she returned home
he did what he had
promised the Lord.

Soon the men of Ephraim
came to Jephthah and said,
"Why did you go fight
the Ammonites without inviting us?"

"I didn't think you guys would help,"
said Jephthah.
This made the men of Ephraim very mad,
and they drew their swords.
But Jephthah and the men of Gilead
struck them all down.
Then they captured the bridge to Ephraim
and whenever an Ephraimite
wanted to cross, they asked,
"Are you an Ephraimite?"

"No way, not me!"
the Ephraimite would reply.

"Well," said the Gideonites,
"say 'Shelly sells sea shells'
quickly thirty times."

"Shelly sells sea shells."

"Selly shells see cells."

"Silly sells she smells . . ."

By that time they were dead.
All in all, forty-two thousand
Ephraimites fell off that bridge—
tripping over their tongues.

THE END

Nuggets from Goldie, the miner prophet:
"Be careful what you promise God."

For the real story, read Judges 10:6–12:7.

MIKE THALER PRESENTS ...

ACTION HEROES OF THE BIBLE

THE SERMONATORS

Life Issue: Sometimes it's hard to do what God wants me to.

Spiritual Building Block: Obedience

Find out why it's worth it to obey:

Think About It:

What would happen if your mom decided that she was sick of stopping at red lights? doubt you'd want to be in the car with her. Just like traffic laws, rules are made to pr tect you and others. It's easy to think that if you're the only one breaking the rule, it' not a big deal. But if everyone thought that way, we'd have big time chaos. Think abc the reason behind the rules you have to follow.

Talk About It:

Grab your dad and get him to help you think of as many people as you can—whethe they be friends, family members, Bible characters, or famous people—who have ha pay a price for disobeying. You'll be amazed at how many there are. If only they had done what they were supposed to, they could have avoided a whole lot of suffering.

Try It:

Make a commitment to yourself to completely follow all the rules at home and scho and everywhere else for a whole week. (If you mess up, just start from where you le off.) See how it feels. After the week is over, think about what might have happened you had broken any rules. Life is just so much more fun when you're doing the righ thing.